Explore the Outdoors

Hunting

Have Fun, Be Smart

By Jack Weaver

The Rosen Publishing Group, Inc.
New York

To the volunteer hunter/trapper education instructors throughout North America, who dedicate their time and energy to educate youth in the fundamentals of hunting and trapping.

Published in 2003 by The Rosen Publishing Group, Inc.
29 East 21st Street, New York, NY 10010

Revised Edition 2003

Library of Congress Cataloging-in-Publication Data

Weaver, Jack.
    Hunting : have fun, be smart / Jack Weaver.
      p.   cm. — (Explore the outdoors)
    Includes bibliographical references and index.
    Summary: Introduces the sport of hunting, its history, equipment, skills, techniques, how to get started, and firearm safety.
    ISBN 0-8239-3760-7
    1. Hunting—Juvenile literature. [1. Hunting.] I. Title. II. Series.
  799.2—dc21
  SK35.5 .W43 2000

                                                                00-021285

Manufactured in the United States of America

Contents

Introduction

At first light you step through a stand of aspens, their leaves golden now in autumn. The air is crisp and your breathing is a small rasp in your throat. A spot you know well is near, up ahead, beyond the narrow meadow separating the forest. An animal path cuts across the open space off to your left, upwind from where you stand. It disappears into the forest, and in your mind's eye you see it winding close to your usual perch.

You carry your bow at your side; there is no prey in sight. Today's hunt will be a waiting game. You are listening, watching, and waiting for sound and movement that will bring one moment of nervous energy which, controlled, could yield tonight's dinner.

A breeze whistles through the aspens, rattling their limbs. You step through the brush thistles to mask your movement behind the sounds of the trees. Stepping through the forest barrier, you find the light dimmer here. It will be many minutes before full light gives definition to wooded outline.

Suddenly you are startled by a chorus of young barn owls, their loud, crazy hooting erupting out of the gloom to your left. Then from a distant ridge comes the deep, hollow rhythm of a great horned owl. You are about to walk toward the blind that you set up weeks ago when a sharper sound comes from the right. This sound is closer, deliberate. You slowly kneel next to a tree, using only your eyes to scan left and right. The sound is not repeated. You wait, looking through the gloom for an outline against the trees. There is nothing.

After a few minutes, you slowly stand and move on. The sound was nothing, but has given you a new edge to take to your perch. Your senses are now heightened. You are aware of yourself and your surroundings. You come to the spot you've found to be so lucky in the past. It's a grouping of only three aspens, thick where they rise from the loamy ground. The spot is hardly a blind, but then a blind will not do for bow hunting. You need to have room to move, to aim, and to see the prey against the forest floor.

Turkey is your prey today, wild turkey of the Rocky Mountains. It is a plentiful bird of the region, but a challenge for any bow hunter. They present a small target in size, and move almost constantly. When spooked, they spank the air with their wings and fly low and fast through the trees. If your arrow doesn't strike on the first shot, you will be left waiting in the cold.

Resting on your knees against the trees, you wait in silence for several minutes. You know gobblers roost up in the trees. You begin to hear them as they rouse from the evening roost.

Then you hear the beat of heavy wings and the crack of twigs breaking as several large birds fly down from the trees. A gobbler talks and beats its wings far ahead—forty yards at least—through the trees. A handful of hens is cackling nearby. You pick up your call and give a couple of soft clucks, trying to sound like an interested hen. You are rewarded by answering gobbles from the bird in front and the one to the right. Now you make two soft yelps. There is an explosion of sound as another gobbler in the trees answers. Later the turkey to your right answers, and it sounds as though he is closer, but moving through the brush to the right.

The calling continues back and forth. Both gobblers are just *out of sight, about thirty yards away. Then you see movement. To your left, two gobblers are coming in from an angle, clucking softly and stopping occasionally to scratch or pick something from the ground. You stay silent behind the trees, hoping they won't spot you and sound an alarm.*

You can hear a turkey walking in the leaves and dragging his wings in full strut. You know he's close. Its scratching feet comes clearly through the brush. You don't move. Moving will cause noise or make you visible. Either will ruin the shot you are hoping to get. This is not a shotgun hunt. You need to wait for the gobbler to get close.

It's time to pull an arrow from your quill and set it in the bow

string. When the turkey comes in sight, you don't want to be fumbling for your weapon. You raise the bow and hold it steady toward the sound you hear in front of you. Your fingers are on the bow string, and then you pull it back and set your wrist against your cheek. The stems of a bush move in jerks. The gobbler is just behind it now. In a moment—yes! The big turkey has come into sight. Your arm screams from the pull of the powerful bow. You set your eye down the arrow shaft against your target. Today is your day!

People today hunt for many different reasons. Some hunters enjoy the challenge of stalking prey. Others hunt for the food the animal will provide. Each hunted prey is a different sport with challenges all its own. Types of hunting include flushing out grouse and woodcock in the eastern woodlands, working pheasants behind a pair of English setters in the Great Plains, shivering in a waterfowl blind along the Atlantic seaboard, stalking moose in the Rocky Mountains, or just searching for squirrels.

Hunting satisfies the desire to be outdoors in a different way than hiking or camping. Hunting requires the mastery of certain basic skills such as marksmanship, woods lore, wildlife knowledge, and tracking. Hunters also need a sense of camaraderie and a high level of outdoor ethics, especially a sense of fair chase. Hunting is a unique privilege that was hard earned, as you will learn in the next chapter. The hunter is rewarded by finally sitting down to enjoy a roast of venison, a brace of ducks, or a dinner with friends of whatever wild game he or she has been fortunate enough to bring home.

Hunting is not for the fainthearted, nor for the careless. Hunting demands respect for the land, respect for the game you hunt, respect for your weapon, respect for others, and even respect for yourself. Each of these is a demanding challenge with rewards of adventures for those who work hard. Success will give cherished memories for a lifetime.

1 Hunting History

Humans began to hunt as soon as they learned how to use simple tools. From the first prehistoric hunters until present day, human beings have hunted for one primary reason: food for survival. Hunting for sport, however, has also become more common within the last few hundred years. This book focuses on the kinds of game and hunting methods that are popular in the Americas.

The Colonial Era (1600s–1780s)

The early American colonies were made up mostly of farmers. They ate some of the grains they grew and the livestock they raised. Mostly, though, they needed to sell their produce for money and goods. Little industry existed that provided the kinds of food markets that we have today. Because wild game was needed for food, the colonists decided that this bounty should belong to everyone, and not just the landowners, as was the case in Europe.

Unfortunately, wildlife and other natural resources were mistakenly thought to be inexhaustible. As pioneers pushed farther into the interior, an explosion of industry followed. Rail-

Hunting in Early Europe

The ancestors of today's hunters had much to contend with. Although wild game such as wild boar, bear, deer, partridge, and rabbit abounded in Europe during medieval times, wild game only belonged to the king and his

ROBIN HOOD

lords and ladies; if you were a commoner, you were not permitted to hunt for food. The penalty for poaching was death. In England, for example, the king's gamekeepers even used leghold traps to catch poachers, who were then slain on the spot—just for killing even a rabbit! That is one of the reasons Robin Hood was an outlaw. He and his band of merry men lived off the king's game.

roads and modern firearms were soon to wreak havoc on America's wildlife resources. Rather than merely providing meat for frontier kitchens, hunting wildlife suddenly became a highly competitive industry. Armed with mass-produced firearms, market hunters shipped boxcar-loads of wild game to markets in the Eastern United States.

Even before the turn of the twentieth century, America's wildlife resources were quickly becoming depleted. In the West, the buffalo and beaver were all but gone. In the East, elk, furbearers, large predators, waterfowl, and flocks of passenger pigeons, so numerous that their migrations had darkened the sky, were also gone. Whitetail deer were so scarce that when a deer track was found, whole communities would get in their buggies and drive out to see it. Flocks of wild turkeys, grouse, and even black bears were making a last stand in a few remote mountain ranges. Even the rugged hills of the Allegheny Mountains, once covered with virgin stands of giant oak, chestnut, white pine, and hemlock, were reduced to eroded, fire-swept ridges by the logger's axe. But by the late 1800s a new breed of hunter was emerging on the American scene. They called themselves sportsmen.

Sport Hunters and Society

In the early days of sport hunting, sportsmen were mostly rich and powerful people. They lamented the loss of the wild game they loved to hunt. They began to work for change. They formed sportsmen's protective associations, and as a result of their lobbying, individual states began to form wildlife agencies. Laws establishing seasons and bag limits on wildlife were enacted, and game wardens were hired to

enforce those laws on behalf of all the citizens. These were not popular laws, and many game wardens were killed by hunters trying to enforce these laws.

In the late 1930s, most state game agencies began to hire wildlife biologists, and a new era of scientific wildlife management was born. Modern wildlife management has been and still is a hard-fought battle against those who would destroy wildlife habitats through pollution and expanded development. Sport hunters have led the fight for wildlife conservation. This may seem like a contradiction, for sport hunters do indeed hunt and kill wildlife. However, they were the first to support laws that would protect wildlife against extinction. The sport hunters of America help pay the bill for wildlife management through hunting license fees, special excise taxes on hunting and fishing equipment, and donations of their time and energy to help wildlife agencies develop wildlife habitats.

Because of the wildlife management efforts of American sport hunters, North America is once again teeming with wildlife. Most wild game species are again plentiful, and in some cases abundant. Still others, like the buffalo and bald eagle, have been rescued from the brink of extinction. Both are now protected from being hunted. Very few animals on the endangered species list are game animals. Nor are they endangered because of sport hunting. Habitat losses due to urbanization and pollution are the key factors in the decline of wildlife species today.

Actually, sport hunting in North America has never been better. Although carefully managed by state game departments, big game of all types is abundant. Upland game birds are plentiful. Waterfowl hunting is very carefully monitored and managed by both the U.S. Fish and Wildlife Service and state wildlife agencies, and today most species of waterfowl are plentiful. With the exception of the eastern farming communities, small game hunting across the United States is relatively good, especially hunting of woodland species.

The Spectrum of Sport Hunting

Today's sportsmen and sportswomen are willing to travel long distances to pursue their sport. Eastern hunters travel west in pursuit of Rocky Mountain elk, bighorn sheep, mountain goats, antelope, mule deer, and mountain lions. Hunters gunning for ring-necked pheasants chase their prey in the Great Plains. Waterfowl hunters pursue ducks and geese in the pothole country of the Midwest or along

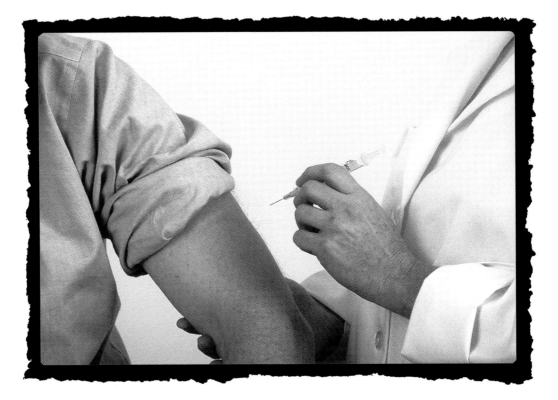

the major flyways. Brown bears, grizzlies, caribou, and Dall sheep are found in Alaska. Northern whitetails, caribou, and moose are hunted in the Canadian provinces, while big racked whitetails are sought in Texas, along with wild hogs.

Nowadays more hunters than ever before are packing their bags and traveling to ever more exotic places. Hunting trips are routinely booked to nearly all parts of the world, including South America, Asia, Australia, Russia, Africa, and the Arctic, in pursuit of everything from big cats to musk ox. But one doesn't just hop on a plane and fly off to exotic places. Passports and visas are needed. So are lots of immunization shots. Ouch! In addition, a reputable outfitter who is familiar with such things as endangered species, hunting licenses, and importation laws is a must. Good outfitters will not only make your trip run smoother and know how to find the game, but they can also keep you out of foreign jails.

For Starters

Beginning hunters should try learning the sport closer to home. For example, try hunting for rabbits or squirrels on a nearby woodlot, farm, or ranch. Many farmers allow hunters to use their woodland properties to hunt small game for a modest fee. As a beginner, this will allow you to become familiar with simple firearms such as the common .22 caliber rifle. Dove or upland game bird hunting is also a sport for beginners who need to gain some experience before taking a trip into the big woods in pursuit of more challenging game. Before you can get started, however, you will need to know what kinds of equipment are available, and which is the best to use for the game you will hunt.

2 The Hunter's Equipment

Beginner sport hunters often find choosing the right weapon difficult. Consider a shotgun, for example. Should you choose a mule-kicking 10 gauge, a 12 gauge, a 16 gauge, 20 gauge, 28 gauge, or the snappy little 4.10, which is really a caliber and not a gauge? Next, do you want a semiautomatic, a pump action, bolt action, hinged action, double barrel, or single barrel? After deciding what type of shotgun you want, you may choose from several brands, depending on your budget. Of course, you should choose a properly choked barrel or barrels for your shotgun. Then come the decisions about ammunition. What size shot? What type of shot? What brand of shot? Or maybe you want rifled slugs instead? Actually it all depends on what you intend to hunt. Understanding some simple basics helps.

The Best Firearm for the Hunt

The first major choice the beginner must make is the type of game he or she would like to hunt. The firearm you will use depends entirely upon the game you intend to hunt. Actually, there are only two types of sporting arms—rifles and shotguns. The difference is inside their barrels. A rifle barrel has grooves

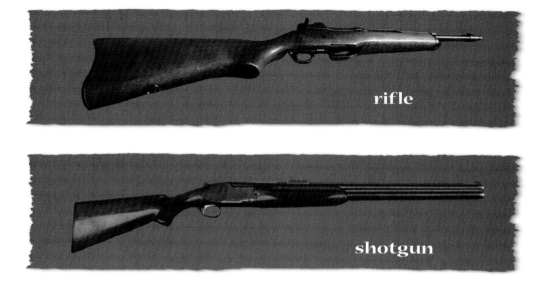

rifle

shotgun

cut inside. These grooves twist around the length of the rifle's barrel. Their purpose is to cause the bullet to spin or spiral much like the spin a quarterback puts on a football when he throws it. This allows the bullet to travel farther and be more accurate.

A shotgun's barrel, on the other hand, is perfectly smooth inside. Unlike a rifle, which fires one bullet at a time, a shotgun generally shoots a charge of small round pellets called shot. This is why shotgun size is measured by gauge, which relates to the size of the shot charge that a particular shotgun is capable of handling. A rifle is measured by caliber, which is a measurement of the diameter of the bullet it can fire.

There are always exceptions to every rule, and as we mentioned earlier, the little 4.10 shotgun is actu-ally a caliber. Generally, however, the smaller the gauge, the bigger the diameter of the shotgun's barrel and the larger the shot charge it can fire. For rifles the opposite is true. The smaller the caliber, the smaller the bullet a particular rifle will fire.

So a .22 caliber rifle and a 20-gauge shotgun are good for beginners because they are easier to handle and have less recoil (kickback).

Ammunition

Ammunition must be handled carefully and with respect for what it can do. A little .22 bullet can travel up to a mile and a half. High-powered rifle and even pistol ammunition can travel much farther. Although most shotgun ammunition is designed for shorter distances—generally under fifty yards—the shot pattern can travel much farther. In addition, bullets do not always stop when they hit something. Often they will pierce through their target and continue on. Shooters must be aware of these simple ballistics and be sure there is a proper backstop behind their targets in order to protect other people and property.

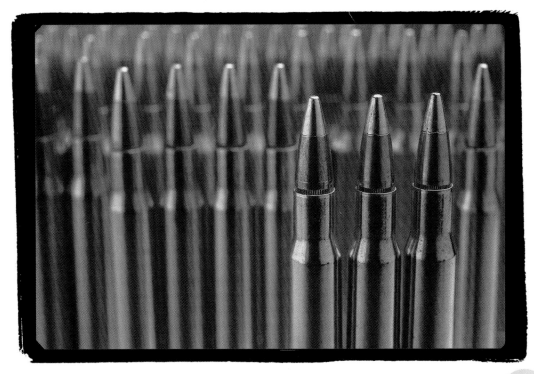

The type of ammunition you need will depend on the firearm and the quarry, or game, you intend to hunt. In the case of shotgun ammo, the size of the shot loads, meaning how big the pellets are inside the shell, will also depend on the size of your quarry. Shot loads of sizes nine to seven and a half are generally used for quail, doves, or grouse. The carton the ammunition comes in will usually explain what game the shot size is effective for. Again, depending on the game you are hunting, you might choose lead, tin, bismuth, or steel shot pellets. Also, be sure to match the caliber of rifle ammunition with the caliber of the firearm. Rifle ammunition is manufactured with different power loads and bullet tips designed for specific game species. Check with a reputable sporting goods dealer

who deals with firearms and ammunition to purchase the correct match.

A sharp knife is also necessary equipment for the hunter. In the case of knives, bigger is not always better. A knife with a blade no longer than four inches is fine. Buy a brand-name knife that is known for holding a keen edge. A dull knife is useless. When considering knives, look for a folding knife with a locking blade. A folding knife is safer and easier to carry, and the blade should lock in place when extended to prevent it from snapping shut on your fingers.

Sport Hunting Clothes

There is a lot of outdoor clothing available for today's hunters. For certain types of hunting, some states require specific amounts of bright orange must be visible at all times. Before you purchase clothing, check the hunting regulations for the area you intend to hunt. But whether you are looking for the latest in camouflage design or the brightest safety clothing, remember that you are going outdoors. Dress for the weather. Most hunting is generally done during the fall and winter. In northern climates layered clothing is best. The outer garment should be water resistant or waterproof. In warmer climates clothing that breathes will allow a free flow of air and help to prevent overheating. This type of clothing will also dry faster should you encounter a surprise shower or fall into a swamp. Generally speaking, blue jeans are not the best clothing to wear in the outdoors, especially when hunting. Good boots, however, are a must. Purchase the best you can afford. Waterproof is best, especially in colder weather. Hunting boots should extend over the ankles for good support in unstable terrain. They should have a rugged sole for traction

and wear. You will probably be out in all kinds of weather, and your boots should be comfortable yet rugged enough to handle it. Your feet are your transportation. If you treat your feet well, they will treat you well. There is nothing worse than wet, cold, and sore feet.

Maps

Maps are important to hunters. Often hunters will need to walk through unfamiliar forests, plains, and mountain trails. A good topographical map of the area a hunter plans to cover can help him or her from getting lost. These maps give detailed information about everything from roads, trails, streams, and buildings to terrain elevation and the types of vegetation you may encounter. Also essential is a compass or a global positioning system (GPS).

Local topographical maps, compasses, and even GPSs can usually be purchased at sporting goods stores. A global positioning system is a handheld computer that works with a navigational satellite to pinpoint the user's location on Earth. GPS cost considerably more than a compass.

Hunting License

Every state in America and each Canadian province requires that hunters buy and carry a hunting license. Requirements for purchasing a hunting license vary between the states, including resident and nonresident requirements. Other considerations include age requirements for junior licenses, whether a junior hunter must be accompanied by an adult, and hunter education requirements for beginners. You may also have to purchase a variety of required licenses, such as big

or small-game tags or specific species stamps. Be sure to check with your state's wildlife agency for licensing details.

Why So Many Requirements Just to Hunt?

The requirements mentioned here aren't as bad as they seem. For starters, you may be able to borrow a firearm from a family member or a friend. Be sure to have a borrowed firearm checked by someone knowledgeable about guns to be sure it is safe and that it functions properly. Ammunition isn't all that expensive, and most of the clothes used for hunting may also be worn for other outdoor pursuits, such as hiking, camping, or fishing. One good thing about hunting is that you may pursue the sport in one fashion or another year-round. If the hunting season isn't open, go hiking. Walk around the area you intend to hunt and become familiar with the lay of the land, what animals live there, and where they get their

Your Survival Kit

Hunters should carry some sort of survival kit while hunting. Sporting-goods stores stock survival kits that hold the basic needs should an emergency occur. A good survival kit should contain some basic first-aid items, a whistle, material for making a shelter, a small flashlight, extra food, and fire starting materials, including waterproof matches.

food. This is called scouting. If most of the wild land near you is posted against trespassing, you need to get permission from the landowner first. You'll find more on this subject in chapter 5. If you don't have easy access to huntable land, remember that half the fun of hunting is learning about wildlife. So get outdoors as much as possible and start looking for wildlife. Even the biggest city has wild animals living in it. If there is grass, trees, or water, there is wildlife. You may be surprised at what you find. Be careful, but don't forget to have fun!

3 The Way of the Hunter

Hunters catch game using many methods. Most hunting requires that the hunter get pretty close to game in order to get off a good shot. Sometimes hunters are closer than fifty yards. This chapter looks at calling, stalking, and other methods of getting close to your game.

Calling Your Game

Many species of game may be hunted by calling. In the case of turkeys, this means trying to imitate a hen in the spring or a lost member of the flock during the fall. Ducks and geese are generally called within the close range necessary for shotguns by trying to imitate the feeding sounds of other waterfowl. Still other game may be called in close by imitating the fighting sounds that male rivals make during breeding season. Bucks, for example, may be called within bowshot range by rattling antlers and using a grunt call. Bull elk and moose sometimes respond to the challenging bugles of their kind with explosive action. Predators such as coyotes and foxes may be called by imitating their quarry's distress calls or the distress calls of one of their young. Crows may also be called in this fashion. The list doesn't end here. Although anyone can do it, learning to call game successfully takes considerable practice and patience. However, it is one of the most exciting and satisfying methods of hunting there is.

Stalking

Stalking may be the most common method of hunting. Stalking is done as it sounds: a hunter walks slowly and quietly through the woods looking for game. The key here is to know where your quarry is likely to be at any given time. You wouldn't want to be stalking through the high country if all the elk are in the lowlands. This is where preseason scouting and knowing your quarry come in handy. If you are after deer, for example, you will need to learn their feeding habits, where their feeding areas are, and when they move into or away from their feeding areas. You must also know where they are likely to shelter during stormy weather and where their bedding or resting areas are. For the restless hunter, stalking is a good technique.

Stand Hunting

Stand hunting is popular, but it can be misleading for the beginner. Hunting from a stand, whether it is a portable tree stand, some type of permanent stand, or just a favorite spot, depends upon the natural movements of wildlife to work. Animal movement patterns vary over time because the woods are in a constant state of change. Just because someone has bagged a deer on a particular stand for the past ten years doesn't mean that spot will continue to produce. Again, scouting the area you intend to hunt is a must. Look for game trails, buck rubs or scrapes, droppings, and

the availability of food. You'll learn more about tree stands in the next chapter.

Driving Game

For certain types of hunting, driving game is by far the most productive method. Driving game generally involves several hunters working together, although small drives can be done by as few as two hunters. When driving, a hunting party is divided into two groups, drivers and watchers. It is the drivers' job to get the game moving by traveling through the woods in a sort of skirmish line. The watchers are positioned at strategic points where the game is expected to go. Obviously, this takes a good deal of cooperation on the part of everyone involved and requires some serious safety considerations. It is an effective technique, especially if you are hunting for whitetailed deer.

Bow Hunting

Hunting using a bow and arrow predates written history. Prehistoric cave drawings show people using bows and arrows to hunt animals such as deer and bison. Before the invention of gunpowder and the use of rifles for hunting, many societies used the accurate method of bowhunting to bring meat to the group.

The bow and arrow is an ingenious invention. Basically, a flexible wooden rod is rigged with a taught string that, when pulled back, creates a great force. This force shoots arrows much faster and farther than the human arm can throw a spear, knife, or rock. The arrow's ability to pierce tough animal hide when shot from the

bow has helped small and large societies to feed themselves throughout the long winters when no crops can be grown and harvested. Bowhunting became a great tool that has helped humans survive for thousands of years.

Modern Bowhunting Equipment

Bowhunting today uses the latest in materials and engineering technology. Bows are made of fiberglass or graphite materials. Compound bows have wheels fitted on the ends of both the top and bottom bow limbs. These wheels act as a pully system to create greater tension when the string is pulled back. Compound bows provide faster arrow speed and longer flying distance. Both give hunters a better chance against swift animals such as deer and rabbit.

The best feature of the compound bow, however, has to do with how much strength an archer needs to pull back the string. The string at full draw has a force (called the draw weight) equal to forty-five pounds. When an archer draws a compound bow string, the draw weight applies its greatest force at the halfway point. After the halfway point, the draw weight decreases dramatically to full draw. This enables archers to hold their aim longer, increasing aiming accuracy and the chance for a more precise shot.

Bowhunting for Game

Bowhunters can hunt both small and large game. Blunt headed arrows are used to hunt rabbit, grouse, hare, and squirrel. Bowfishing is also a popular sport. Barbed arrows tied to a string enable hunters to hook and reel in game fish such as trout, bass, and even shark! Bowhunters can

also bring down big game, including elk, hogs, moose, deer, and turkey. Regulations exist in each state on when and how game can be hunted. You should always check state regulations before you begin each hunting season.

Bowhunters hunt either by stalking game or stand hunting, which were both explained earlier. Bow hunting equalizes the challenge between hunters and prey. Bowhunters must be swift, steady, and silent, or else they will get no prey. If you are looking for a challenge when you hunt, then bowhunting is probably for you.

4 Safety First!

Learning to hunt is a lot like learning to drive a car. There is no place for a reckless or irresponsible person behind the wheel of an automobile, and the same holds true for hunting. Irresponsible actions with a firearm can kill or cause serious injury to people and property. For this reason almost every state requires first-time hunters to complete a hunter education course sponsored by the state's wildlife agency. An identification card is issued to each successful graduate. This card must then be presented when purchasing a hunting license.

Today, hunter education courses are being standardized throughout the United States. Qualified volunteers, under the supervision of state wildlife agencies, teach the courses. Courses generally require a minimum of ten hours or more to complete.

Hunter Education Courses

Today's hunter education courses include firearm handling and safety, ammunition identification and use, firearm safety in the home, hunter responsibility, game identification, survival, first aid, ethics, landowner relations, game laws, archery, muzzle loading, and much, much more.

Most courses teach marksmanship and shooting fundamentals by offering live firing on ranges under the supervision of qualified range masters. Many also offer mock hunts that walk students through actual field courses. Some states offer home study courses—some with CD-ROM interactive scenarios. The purpose of home study is to give busy students the opportunity to complete the academic portion of the course at home. After successfully completing the written portion of the course, students then must complete the practical, hands-on portion under the supervision of course instructors.

To find out how to register for a hunter education course, contact your state wildlife agency, local sportsman's club, or inquire at gun shops and sporting-goods stores in your area.

The Basic Rules

Actually, hunter safety, like any safety issue, involves applying common sense when in the field. Hunter education identifies and then clarifies these safety issues for the beginner and experienced hunter alike. Three basic rules of firearm safety sum it up best. Plant them firmly in your mind, and follow them as though they were written in stone. That way, you can truly have fun and be smart!

Tree Stand Safety

Tree stand safety is one of the leading issues in hunting circles today. On a nationwide average, more people are injured, some fatally, by falling from tree stands than through

Three Basic Rules for Hunting Safety

1. Treat every firearm as if it were loaded! Every firearm must be treated with respect. Assume every gun is loaded until you personally look into the action (those parts that load and fire a gun) to be sure it is not.

2. Always keep the muzzle pointed in a safe direction! The muzzle is the end of a firearm where the bullets exit. Always keep the muzzle of your firearm pointed in a safe direction—away from others. That way, should the gun be set off accidentally, no one will be hurt.

3. Be sure of your target! Legal game is the only target any hunter should be shooting at. Double-check your target before you pull the trigger!

firearm mishaps. The danger comes from standing on curved tree limbs, sometimes wet and slippery, while holding a firearm. When the shotgot or rifle kicks, it can easily make a hunter move his or her feet. Then—pow!—a slip and fall down through the rough limbs to the ground. The majority of these accidents are preventable, and hunters should never go aloft without attaching themselves securely to the tree with a safety harness.

5 Let's Get Started!

So you want to go hunting? Well, OK. Deciding to do it is the first big step. Taking a hunter education course is the second. Having done that, you will need a firearm or bow and arrows. Assuming you've already decided on what you want to hunt and the type of gun you need, all that remains is to obtain your firearm.

There is one consideration, however: Are you of legal age to own firearms? Federal law prohibits persons under eighteen from purchasing or owning a shotgun or rifle, and prohibits those under twenty-one from purchasing or owning a handgun. (This federal law also prevails over state laws.) It isn't necessary to purchase a new sporting firearm if the price is a problem. Just about every gun shop sells both new and used firearms.

If you are purchasing a used firearm, make sure you buy it from a reputable gun shop that checks used firearms thoroughly before offering them for resale to ensure they are working properly and are safe. If you are going to borrow one from a relative, neighbor, or friend, have it checked by someone familiar with that type of firearm to be sure it is safe before shooting it. More than one gun has exploded in the shooter's hands because someone accidentally left a cleaning patch inside the barrel. Especially check the safety mechanism (the part that blocks the trigger from firing prematurely) to be sure that it is working properly.

Mentoring

Traditionally, hunting has been handed down from father to son as a part of a family's traditions. Today that has changed. For one thing, more women are becoming involved in hunting and other forms of outdoor recreation. For many reasons, however, hunting is not being pursued as actively as it once was, which is good for those who do hunt because more hunting opportunities are opening up. These are great times to be hunting! But it may be a little difficult for a beginner to find a mentor, especially since many parents no longer hunt.

Having a mentor to show you the way is important. It's sort of like having a pro baseball player teach you how to play ball. If your mom or dad is a nonhunter, let your friends and relatives who do hunt know that you are interested in learning about hunting. Often they will take you under their wing, so to speak. After all, they know the ropes and maybe even belong to a hunting camp somewhere. If your relatives don't hunt, ask friends of the family, but don't just grab anybody. Make sure your prospective mentor is a trustworthy and responsible person. Would you want someone who drives under the influence of drugs or alcohol to teach you about driving? I hope not! Anyway, you get the idea. If you have a local hunter's organization or shooting club that is active in your area, you might also check to see if they have youth programs or youth memberships. Then get involved with their group and group projects. A

Other Options

For now, perhaps the very first thing you need to do is find out if hunting is really for you. Obviously you have an interest in outdoor recreation or you wouldn't be reading this book. But are you sure you are interested in hunting, or could your interest lean more toward camping, boating, fishing, hiking, or outdoor photography? Of course, you may combine any of those sports with hunting. The only way to find out, though, is to learn all you can about hunting first. There are lots of good books available about hunting. Check some out at the library. There are also several national magazines that feature hunting articles and stories. Also, check with your state wildlife agency. Most wildlife agencies publish a monthly conservation magazine that features hunting articles and articles about wildlife. All wildlife agencies have helpful books, brochures, and handouts. Most publish wildlife videos, which may be purchased inexpensively.

hunting group can be a good place to find a mentor for hunting and to learn to shoot as well.

Look Around

Finally, if you can, just get out in the woods. Walk around quietly and look for animals and animal signs. But be careful! At first, go someplace that is familiar to you so you don't get lost. Or go to a state park until you become used to making your way around in the outdoors. Go outside during different seasons of the year to see if you're really going to enjoy being out in all kinds of weather. Not everyone does. Also, choose your hiking companions wisely. It is not fun to be in the woods with someone who complains about insects, cobwebs, dirt, or snakes. You should learn what kinds of animals to stay away from—such as rattlesnakes, for example. Learn how to avoid areas where these critters may be found until you become comfortable dealing with such situations safely. If you respect the outdoors, the outdoors will respect you. Remember, respect is always earned.

Finally, always let someone know where you are going and when you plan to return. Give them a specific description of the area, such as the name of a hollow or a canyon. That way, if you don't return within a reasonable period of time, they will know where to look or where to send search parties. After all, it is very easy to fall, break a leg, or sprain an ankle in the woods. Common sense and good judgment should always prevail when you're in the great outdoors.

6 Learning Basic Skills

Marksmanship and other skills needed for hunting must be learned and developed, like the skills of any other sport. Hunting and shooting do not require a high degree of athletic ability. However, learning how to shoot requires an understanding of the fundamentals of marksmanship. As we already mentioned, taking a hunter education course will help get you started, but you still need to practice to become a skilled marksman. Target practice, therefore, becomes a necessary activity.

Starting Target Practice

Just setting out some tin cans or pinning up a paper target and blazing away is not the best way to learn. First, safety precautions must be taken. Remember to build a backstop to keep your bullets from traveling beyond the target. A beginner definitely needs the supervision of an experienced adult marksman. Joining a hunter's club is one way to accomplish this, since most clubs have some type of safe shooting facilities available for their members. Another way might be to join a National Rifle Association shooting team. There you will get the valuable assistance of trained coaches.

For the competition-minded, there are lots of fun ways to develop and hone those skills needed to become a successful hunter. A few are listed below.

Small-bore rifle (.22 caliber)

Competition in this category involves shooting at paper targets at different ranges and in different positions, such as lying down, sitting, and standing. Shooting may be done at indoor or outdoor ranges. This is the best way for beginners to learn the basics of marksmanship.

High-powered rifle

These competitions are held at outdoor ranges. They may be very formal in terms of competition rules and conduct, or they may be casual, such as the type often conducted by local sportsmen and sportswomen. But whether formal or casual, the strict observance of range safety rules is always in order. High-powered rifle contestants may shoot from a bench rest at paper targets at ranges anywhere from 100 yards to 1,000 yards or more. Some contests involve shooting at moving targets from off-hand standing positions. Some, such as the long-range competitions, require telescopic sights, while others may specify iron or open sights only.

Muzzle loader and black powder

These competitions are generally held using primitive-type firearms such as flintlock rifles. Many black powder shoots are gala events with the participants dressing in frontier or mountaineer clothing. Often shooting is done off-hand, but some matches are only done with heavy bench-rest target rifles. Novelty shooting is a hallmark of these events. One event involves shooting a soft lead ball at the edge of an axe that cuts the ball in two, hopefully, causing each piece to break a balloon on either side of the blade. Tomahawk and knife throwing are regular features at such competitions. Early American camps are usually set up at such events, and visitors are encouraged to tour and speak with the participants. This gives folks a real-life history lesson about early America that will not soon be forgotten.

Archery

Archery shooting may be done using many targets, from traditional bull's-eyes to Styrofoam models of game animals. Field archery courses involve shooting at replicas of game animals under actual field conditions. For example, contestants may walk through a wooded trail and shoot at targets set up at different ranges or even shoot from tree stands. Also, many archery shops now offer indoor archery competitions. They simulate actual hunting situations with electronic machines that project hunting scenes onto a blue-screen background, like on T.V.

Trap and skeet shooting

This is traditional shotgun shooting at its best. With trap, shooters take up a position behind a low structure that houses a clay bird–throwing machine. When the shooter is ready, he or she yells "Pull!" A clay disk is released and the shooter tries to break it in the air. Disks are released at various speeds, angles, and heights. The shooter who breaks the most wins.

Skeet is a little different, in that a group of shooters stand in a semicircle. Two trap houses sit to the right and left of the shooters' positions. One is high and one low. Clay birds are thrown across the front of the shooters in combinations of singles, doubles, or triples. The shooters rotate through the five firing positions to alter their perspective.

Shooting sporting clays where real hunting situations are simulated is an ever more popular type of shotgun-shooting competition. Clay bird traps are set up and hidden in a variety of actual field conditions, such as in a thick aspen wood or beside a pond. Each station simulates a different type of hunting scenario. Various sizes of clay disks are used to imitate different types of game. Some bounce along the ground like a cottontail rabbit would, while others sail through the thick brush or come right at the shooter the way a grouse or dove might. Still others flush straight up like a pheasant or a mallard. This is the most realistic type of shotgun shooting there is, and it's fun!

Competition: Getting Involved

The National Rifle Association sponsors one of the best competitions for young people through a program called Youth Hunter Education Challenge. Although the competition is open to single contestants, local sportsmans clubs usually cosponsor the program. Regional, state, and national championships are conducted annually. This competition involves outdoor rifle, shotgun, and archery shooting at simulated game animals under actual field conditions. The competition also involves a written test of hunter education principles, ethics, and a general knowledge of safety-related issues. A hunter safety trail offers contestants a hands-on test of game identification, survival skills, and compass orienteering.

There are many other kinds of shooting sports competitions, including handguns, and combat shooting. Many state and national organizations offer special incentive programs for youths interested in hunting, including the National Wild Turkey Association's Jake's Day event. Youth Field Day events are offered in several states at local sportsman's clubs. Check the listings at the back of this book for sources that will help connect you with these and other skill-developing games and competitions.

7 Hunting Pros and Cons

"Hunting is cruel. It is deceitful. It is socially unjustifiable," says one of the United States's leading antihunting lobbying groups.

"Sportsmen and sportswomen are America's greatest conservationists," claims one of America's prominent conservation organizations.

In our society, people hold many different opinions regarding the treatment of animals. Some people object to any practice that involves the killing or using of animals for medical research. Others, such as those in one leading anti-hunting organization, claim that hunters take a heavy toll on endangered and threatened species.

However, when considering the pros and cons of hunting, it is important to get all the facts. In the case of hurting endangered species, hunters are required to pay to protect threatened and endangered species. Hunters provide millions of dollars per year in the United States in the form of special taxes on hunting equipment, licenses, and permits. This money is used to manage both protected and huntable species, such as the sea otter, the bald eagle, and the peregrine falcon have been brought back from the brink of extinction with the aid provided by this tax money.

Another important part of getting the facts about hunting is looking critically at advertising campaigns. Many antihunting campaigns are visible and well-funded. Wildlife agencies, on the other hand, do not necessarily spend their money on publicity programs that defend hunting.

The question of hunting is really more of an emotional and moral issue than an environmental issue. This is where your own personal belief system comes into play. The key is to consider all of the factors, and then to decide for yourself.

Hunting means taking the life of an animal, and you have to feel comfortable with that. Talk to hunters in your family or community about how they view their role. You will probably find that they have respect for the wildlife they hunt. You may also find that hunting in your area actually helps to control problems of animal overpopulation.

If you decide that hunting is not for you, that is OK. If friends or family expect you to hunt, you can explain to them exactly why it is not for you. Whatever your reason, people should respect your decision.

A Final Word for Young Hunters

Each hunter must assume personal responsibility for his or her sport. Hunters must always ensure that certain principles, such as fair chase, are not violated. They must be committed to obeying all season and bag limits, along with

Help for Hunting Hype

Find out the facts about hunting. Some organizations may be more reputable than others with regard to the information that they publish. Think about hunting from different angles and read a variety of articles in magazines or on the Internet, but don't believe everything that you read!

Most of all, try not to fall into the pattern of condemning someone who disagrees with you regarding "to hunt or not to hunt." It is a complex issue and everyone has an opinion.

all the other regulations that govern hunting. Finally, they must take an active part in helping to police their own ranks by taking a strong stand against poaching and other wildlife crime. Sportsmen and sportswomen should never be shy about reporting those who deliberately violate the rules of their sport. As hunters who follow the rules, it is their duty.

If hunters do these things and hunt responsibly, our society will continue to support hunting as a viable recreational activity.

Glossary

Action
The parts of a firearm that load and fire a gun.

Backstop
An object designed to safely stop a projectile fired from a gun, bow, or crossbow on a target range.

Bait
Food or other enticement used to lure wild game to within shooting range.

Blinds
Simple shelters used to conceal a hunter from wild game.

Bow
A handheld device used to shoot arrows.

Buck Rubs
Small trees or saplings that have been shredded or scraped by a buck's antlers.

Buckshot
Shot shells containing large shot sizes, which are used mostly for big game.

Caliber

The diameter of a bullet or the inside diameter of a rifle's barrel.

Calling

A hunting method where a hunter makes sounds that imitate birds and animals that help draw the game into shooting range.

Camouflage

Materials designed to blend into a wilderness background for concealment.

Cap and Ball

A type of muzzleloading firearm ignition that involves using a primer cap, which ignites the powder charge in the muzzle.

Clay Bird

A clay disk used as a target for shotgun shooting.

Crossbow

A bow fixed crosswise on a stock with a trigger release.

Driving Game

A method of hunting that involves using people to push wild game toward hunters in waiting.

Fair Chase

The concept of allowing game animals to have a fair chance of escape.

Flintlock

primitive ignition system for a muzzleloading firearm. It involves using a piece of flint to send a shower of sparks into a pan of priming powder to ignite the powder in the barrel of the gun.

Game

Wild animals that are hunted for food and sport.

Game Calls
Devices that produce certain sounds that attract animals.

Game Laws
Laws that regulate sport hunting and protect non-huntable species.

Game Tags
Tags that are required by wildlife agencies to place on animal carcasses.

Gauge
The method by which shotgun size and the size of a shot charge are determined.

Global Positioning System (GPS)
Handheld computers that can calculate one's exact position using a global positioning satellite.

Habitat
A place containing all the necessary requirements for a particular species of wildlife to live, such as food, water, shelter, and space.

Habitat Loss
The loss of crucial wildlife habitat, usually to unrestricted human development, such as housing developments, highways, or shopping malls.

Harvest
A term referring to the annual take of surplus game by hunting.

In-Line Muzzle Loader
A modern muzzle loading rifle with the firing mechanism in direct line with the gun's barrel.

Lacy Act
A law that makes the transportation of illegally taken wildlife across state

boundaries a federal felony.

Muzzle Loader

A firearm that requires the powder charge and projectiles to be loaded individually by pushing them down the barrel with a ramrod.

Nonrenewable Resources

Natural resources available in fixed amounts such as coal, oil, and gas.

P-R Funds

A special excise tax levied on sporting arms and ammunition that is used for wildlife restoration and hunter education.

Poaching

Hunting game out of hunting season; also used to describe people who hunt animals on the endangered species list.

Ramrod

A slim rod used to drive a powder charge, patch, and projectile down the barrel of a muzzle loading firearm.

Renewable Resources

Natural resources that reproduce themselves annually, such as wildlife.

Rifle

Firearm with grooves inside the barrel to cause the projectile to spin when fired.

Riffled Slug

Single projectile ammunition for shotguns.

Safety

A blocking device that prevents the trigger from pulling or blocks the firing pin or hammer from striking a chambered shell.

Safety Harness
Safety device used to prevent a hunter from falling out of a tree.

Scrapes
Small area of earth that is scraped by the hooves of a buck during the breeding or rutting season to mark his territory.

Shot String
Shot fired from a shotgun is strung out in a line called a shot string.

Sight
Mechanism used for aiming a firearm, bow, or crossbow.

Small Game
Smaller animals such as squirrels, rabbits, grouse, and pheasants.

Sporting Arm
A firearm used for the purpose of hunting or target shooting.

Stalking
Method of hunting consisting of carefully moving through the woods searching for game or following the trail of a game animal.

Stand
A place where a hunter waits for game, such as in a tree stand.

Still-Hunting
Waiting in one spot for legal game to appear.

Sustained Yield
The goal of regulated hunting. To control the harvest of game animals annually through wildlife law enforcement so each year's harvest does not exceed a wild population's ability to recover.

Topographical Map
A map that includes terrain types and elevations.

Wildlife Conservation
The philosophy of wisely using renewable natural resources.

Wildlife Management
The science of managing wildlife resources.

Resources

Organizations

In the United States

American Hunting Dog Club (AHDC)
Box 145
Cranby, CT 06035
Web site: http://ahdc.org

National Rifle Association
Hunter Services Department
11250 Waples Mill Road
Fairfax, VA 22030
Web site: http://www.nra.org

National Shooting Sports Foundation
Flintlock Ridge Office Center
11 Mile Hill Road
Newtown, CT 06470-2359
Web site: http://www.nssf.org

National Wild Turkey Federation
P.O. Box 530
Edgefield, SC 29824
Web site: http://www.nwtf.org

Canada's Northwest Territories Explorers' Guide
NWT Arctic Tourism
Box 610, Yellowknife, Canada NT X1A 2N5
(867) 873-7200
Web site: http://www.nwttravel.nt.ca

Outdoor Canada
P.O. Box 398
Kingston, Nova Scotia, Canada B0P 1R0
Web site: http://www.outdoor-canada.com

Web Sites

Due to the changing nature of internet links, the Rosen Publishing Group, Inc., has developed an online list of Web sites related to the subject of this book. This site is updated regularly. Please use this link to access the list:

http://www.rosenlinks.com/eou/hunt/

For Further Reading

Books

Christian, Chris. *The Gun Digest Book of Trap and Skeet Shooting*. Iola, WI: Krause Publications, 1994.

Field & Stream: The World of Big-Game Hunting. Minnetonka, MN: Creative Publishing International, 1999.

Lawrence, H. Lea. *The Archer's and Bowhunter's Bible*. New York: Doubleday and Company, 1993.

McIntyre, Thomas. *The Field & Stream Shooting Sports Handbook*. New York: Lyons Press, 1999.

McLead-Everette, Sharon. *Walk Softly With Me: Adventures of a Woman Big-Game Guide in Alaska*. Fairbanks, AK: Vanessapress, 1998.

Murtz, Harold A. *The Gun Digest of Sporting Clays*. Iola, WI: Krause Publications, 1999.

Painter, Doug Hunting. *The Field & Stream Firearms Safety Handbook*. New York: Lyons Press, 1999.

Rue, Leonard Lee. *Deer Hunter's Encyclopedia*. Gilford, CT: Globe Pequot, 2000.

Underwood, LaMar, ed. *Whitetail Hunting Tactics of the Pros.* Gilford, CT: Globe Pequot, 2001.

Valerio, Maurizio. *Big Game Hunting in North America.* Baker City, OR: Picked-By-You Guides, 1999.

Magazines

Blackpowder Hunting

Bow and Arrow Hunting

Deer & Deer Hunting

Field & Stream

Hunting

Fur, Fish and Game

Outdoor Life

Turkey & Turkey Hunting

Index

Credits

About the Author

Jack Weaver is a graduate of the Pennsylvania Game Commission's Ross Leffler School of Conservation. He has served as a wildlife conservation officer for the Pennsylvania Game Commission (PGC) since 1969. He has written extensively for the PGC's official magazine, *Pennsylvania Game News,* and is also the author of *Phantoms of the Woods.* He spent the final six years of his career as the information and education supervisor for PGC's northeast region. Throughout his career, Mr. Weaver worked extensively with Pennsylvania's Hunter Education Program. He retired from the Pennsylvania Game Commission in 1999.

Photo Credits

Series Design

Oliver H. Rosenberg

Layout

Cynthia Williamson